The honest guide to the MBA

What you need to know before you decide on it

Marcel Kotowski

ISBN: 978-0-244-25546-6

PublishNation

www.publishnation.co.uk

Many thanks to my family for love and patience.

JMK for support and continuously challenging my thinking.

And Nahi for giving honest feedback on the draft.

Contents

Who is this guide for? 3

PART I FINDING THE SCHOOL 7

    Types of MBA 10

    Accreditation 17

    Why the school may be more important than the diploma 20

    How to choose a school 22

    Applying 25

    Common worries 29

        Finding the money for the course 29

        Previous experience 39

PART II SCHOOL TIME 41

    First steps 41

    Work with your colleagues 42

    Achieving a balance 44

        Time commitment 47

        Family and social life 48

        Use technology 51

    Finding help 56

YouTube and social media 57

Feeling alone 58

Coping with the avalanche 59

MBA and your career 63

How will the MBA influence my career? 63

Talking a different language 66

What about the 'two-year curse'? 66

Last word 68

Who is this guide for?

University websites are filled with pictures of young people smiling at a whiteboard, beaming with confidence, but there is precious little in terms of feedback from real students. This guide aims to change that reality.

It has been designed for two audiences:

1. Those who are just pondering embarking on the journey and are yet to find an appropriate course.

2. Those who have already decided on a course, or study, and have found themselves unable to manage the pressure.

For that reason, I have separated it into two parts. The first one focuses on selecting the best school, and by that I don't mean going for the top one in charts of the *Financial Times*. I must stress here that my experience comes from the United Kingdom but (apart from the relevance of some accreditation) the worries and struggles about choice are universal.

The second part focuses on managing the workload, and here I share examples from my own life as well as others.

Throughout the guide, I have tried to leave nuggets of 'I wish I had known that' to allow you to avoid the most common mistakes.

I have also included some real-life examples. They are genuine although I changed names and job titles for reasons of confidentiality. The MBA exposed me to wonderful people, and I am sure they will recognise themselves in the stories.

You can flip to any place in the guide, or read it from beginning to end. I expect that certain parts of it will become more relevant as you progress on the MBA journey. It is okay to skip a section and come back later.

Before we start going through some of the aspects and worries attached to the process, you must write down what drove you to think about the MBA in the first place. This is significant, so you must be honest with yourself.

Go on, write it down so you can refer to it later.

You haven't done it yet, have you?

Do it, as this leads to lesson number one: this journey is very real, so you have to put effort into it. So, write down your reasons now.

Thank you.

What you are about to embark on is real indeed. If you allow it, it will change your life and the perspective from which you see the world. This will forever remain something that is achieved by a small percentage of people, and you should rightly be proud of yourself.

I can guarantee that by the time you've finished, the diploma will not matter as much as the fact that suddenly you see the world from a broader perspective.

The path lies ahead of you but, as you are now probably realising, having the diploma will not automatically guarantee you better money and status. If it is not managed properly, it can lead to quite the opposite, so pay attention. If you thought otherwise, then you'd better *really* start paying attention.

- *You will only get as much out of the experience as you want to*

- *What you will take from the MBA is down to you,.*

This should become critical to your way of thinking from now on. If you decide to leave your job and study full-time but have no commitment, you will fail.

The pivotal part of studying for an MBA is learning. I have met people using distance modules who listened to lectures while cycling to work, read articles while eating lunch, and watched video materials in the evening instead of watching a movie.

I will elaborate on time management later.

PART I FINDING THE SCHOOL
Why doing an MBA?

Firstly, before we go into details, you must sit down and write down the reasons why you want to join an MBA course. You have probably discussed this in your head many times but, without writing things down, you may not have allowed yourself time to really reflect.

- *Why do you want to start an MBA?*
- *Why an MBA?*
- *Are you looking for specific knowledge, or do you just want to better yourself?*
- *Why not an MSc or perhaps a PhD?*
- *Are you just following your colleagues, for whom an MBA worked?*
- *Do you personally know anyone who has done one?*

The last point is crucial. Speak to people who have done it and can share their experiences. If you don't know anyone, then look up contacts on LinkedIn (seriously). I would expect most of them to be positively disposed towards answering questions.

If you are looking specifically to join certain circles of senior management, find out which schools they graduated from. We will discuss accreditation separately, but in this instance I am talking about the prestige of the school. If you want to join 'the clique', you should consider following the footsteps of your seniors.

And don't be afraid of being big-headed about the process. If your only goal is to gain theoretical knowledge about management then I must praise your motivation but, at the same time, make you aware that the LARGEST and MOST SIGNIFICANT advantage of the course is the ability to exchange experiences with other managers and leaders. If you achieve the balance correctly, 50% of your learning will come from talking to inspirational characters on the course.

Be thorough when asking yourself why you want to join the MBA. My advice is to go for the most fundamental analysis tool of SWOT. Treat yourself as if you are an investigator trying to get to the bottom of your suspect's (your) line of reasoning.

If you have not heard of SWOT, it's a great place to start so look it up on the internet. At the same time, you've probably already (unknowingly) chosen a type of course that will be best suited to you.

You will find out more in the next chapters.

Types of MBA

If you are still in the phase of trying to understand the MBA world, then this section is for you.

You will come across several different types of MBA The decision about which one to choose is important, so spend time researching them in detail.

General MBA: As you will have already guessed, this is a non-specialised one, and is an excellent option if your experience is limited. You may have had a managerial position for less than five years and need credentials to progress further up the ladder. If that's the case, you will do well to focus on that option.

The general MBA aims to equip you with a wide range of skills that are applicable in most sectors. By the time you finish, you will have covered Marketing, Finance, Organisational Behaviour. A lot of programmes offer elective modules should you want to enhance your understanding of a particular subject.

As to the pros and cons of this type of MBA, these depend on where you work now and your goals. Personally, I don't think there are any downsides to whichever option you take, but if you are still in the process of designing your career you'll do well with this option. Going for specialisation boosts your expertise, but if you are a generalist this type of MBA is worth considering.

Executive MBA: These are often known as EMBA. The basic profile of a candidate for this type of MBA is of an experienced individual whose next seat should be in the boardroom. A typical student will already have held several senior positions and be looking for a set of leadership-focused tools to propel them to the c-suite. Do not be surprised if your fellow students are in their forties or older!

Here is an important note for those who think they can join EMBAs from a junior-management level: much of the course involves networking with fellow students around case studies and you may be severely challenged if you cannot contribute on an equal basis. I met one alumnus of such a course who was quite bitter about his experience and doubted himself throughout because the course didn't allow him to grow adequately. Furthermore, he did not progress in his career.

On the other hand I know several managing directors who, thanks to EMBAs, advanced from their previous positions of operation and finance directorships straight into the leading chair. Without exception, all of them were formidable people and praised the EMBA as a phenomenal experience.

My MBA colleague summarised it perfectly when he stated, 'judge your strengths realistically'.

Specialist MBA: No points for guessing what these are about. Typically, the first few modules will resemble those of a general MBA, then the material will focus on a particular subject such as Human Resources, Biotechnology or Finance. These are a fantastic fit for those who know what they want and have a clear idea about the type of industry they want to work in, or are already working in.

A word of warning for those of you who want to choose this option to change your career path: your tutors, who are experts in their fields, will assume you already have a good understanding of the subject and the depth of the study will be significant. For those not familiar with the subject matter, a specialist MBA can prove highly challenging and time-consuming.

If you have little experience and believe you still ought to pursue this path, be prepared for some extra work to understand the basics. My background has always been technical and operations but I went for the Finance option, which pushed my studying time to its limits. In short, go for it if you think you need it – but be realistic and prepared.

William started his MBA course as Head of Operations for one of the largest cosmetic companies in the world. As he was looking to progress into the boardroom he decided on the Finance specialisms, but discovered as he studied that he was more interested in Human Resources (HR). After talking to his university tutor and taking advice from his senior colleagues, he went with HR. Two months before submitting his dissertation, he changed his career by ninety degrees and became a Lead Business Developer in a major FMCG company, in a role focused on identifying and developing future managers.

You may say that William's example shows a lack of progression but what was not mentioned was that he had realised he would be in the boardroom anyway and wanted to achieve that while doing something he enjoyed.

The specialist option will not automatically make you a world-renowned expert, but it will give you a clear plan on how to become one. It can be a double-edged sword when looking for a new job, so make sure your choice does not restrict you in the future.

Once you have a good understanding of the type of MBA you want, the next option is the format. There are effectively four choices.

Full time – suitable for those who can afford to take a break from work. These are intense but can be done in two years in North America, and between twelve and eighteen months in Europe. If you aim to complete in one year, be prepared to switch off your career and almost everything else during that time. You will not have holidays, time for the pub or games with your mates. If you're a dedicated person, however, this option means that you are out of work only for a year.

Be very specific when choosing a school and visit it before you sign up. If you have ten years' experience in running a department, you will suffer if you end up in a class of fresh graduates – but that could be an advantage if you are looking to refresh your point of view and focus on new methods. Go back to the basics and ask yourself what the aim of the MBA is.

Part time – varies between schools, from attending a few weeks every six months to weekends only. This is great if you have a flexible work pattern that allows you to disappear from the office for extended periods. There are many strengths to this option.

If you have enough time in your life, you will definitely benefit from weekly interaction with fellow students. Your workload may be spread between weekend workshops, with homework to complete during the week and contributions to Blackboard, assignments and participation in classes.

Executive – typically take place at weekends and nights on various campuses, most likely spread across different countries. While visiting suppliers in North Africa, I met one student who, having just returned from a seminar in Germany, was preparing for a weekend with the class in Austria. You have to be prepared to mould your life around the course but this story shows the high-profile of the attendees.

Distance learning – this is the most flexible format, in which you will be required to attend a certain number of 'synchronous' (live) online hours per week but can otherwise spread your workload.

A word of warning here: you will still have to put in around 15–20 hours minimum every week, in addition to attending the university at least once a year (generally for a week or a couple of weekends), so don't treat distance learning as 'I study **if** I can' but more 'I study **whenever** I can'.

Accreditation

So far we have covered types and formats of MBAs, but there is a third important factor when looking for the right course: accreditation. The three main forms are:

AACSB: The Association to Advance Collegiate Schools of Business, founded in 1916. It is worth noting that not all members are accredited, and the standard does not include for-profit schools. There are more than 840 schools worldwide certified to this standard.

AMBA: The Association of MBAs in the United Kingdom. I would say that this is a must for UK students as the accreditation body has been active since 1967 and is present in more than seventy countries. They will regularly email you updates on quality events and seminars to make sure you maintain that tip-top MBA level.

EQUIS: The EFMD Quality Improvement System is used in the European Union. It runs under auspices of the European Foundation for Management Development (EFMD) and has more than 170 institutions in forty-one countries around the world.

It is worth mentioning that only ninety MBA schools worldwide (out of more than 13,000) hold all three of these accreditations in an achievement known as the Triple Crown. This may seem strange but there is a good reason for it. There are various requirements for each of the standards, such as levels of internalisation, content, qualitative and quantitive focus on the course, or prescribed faculty ratios, but the most common reason is the previous experience required.

For example, to comply with AMBA, the candidate must have had three years' work experience. Some very prestigious schools, such as Harvard Business School, Wharton, Columbia Business and Stanford, simply don't comply with that requirement. They remain firmly in the forefront of the MBA list due to their reputations that have been forged by the quality of their courses, so you have to achieve a balance when looking at accreditation and the university's reputation.

You may find that some of the universities incorporate additional courses within the MBA, so you may graduate with extra qualifications. For instance, upon successful completion of my class, the university offered CMI (Chartered Management Institute) Level 7 Certificate or Diploma in Management and Leadership.

There are other certification bodies, such as:

DETC: The Distance Education and Training Council which operates in the USA and scrutinises distance-learning courses.

Regional accreditations: Some states in the USA have their own standards, which may not be recognised in other countries. I advise extra caution when looking at these.

Others: You may see other accreditations in university prospectuses; it is impossible to cover all of them in this guide. The advice here is to do your research. You now know which standards are the most recognisable, so you will have to find out whether others are relevant in your industry.

Doing your homework is critical; don't just glance at a prospectus. Make sure that the course is accredited to at least one of the standards. I rejected all non-accredited courses as a waste of time and money when I was looking for my business school.

Why the school may be more important than the diploma

It may surprise you, but your future employer may never see your diploma. Someone in Human Resources may ask you for a copy for the records, but it will not matter to your next boss. It will matter even less if you work for yourself.

You're studying the MBA to gain knowledge, not a diploma. Those who approach that goal differently benefit less from the process and effectively waste a few years of their life and someone else's time.

The best knowledge will be delivered by top specialists in their fields; ideally, you want a healthy mix of academics and practitioners. Those of the highest calibre are typically concentrated in good schools. Of course, this means higher costs.

When looking at possible schools in the UK, you should be aware of the existence of the Russell Group, a self-selecting association of the top twenty-four universities. Why should you look at them? Firstly, more than 75% of all university research grants and contract income in the UK goes to them, which means they have the best researchers and focus on quality. Yes, Cambridge is there – but also schools such as the Universities of Sheffield or Cardiff. Your employer may not know the specifics of the course you selected and not ask for your diploma, but he or she will most likely have heard of the Russell Group. This may have a significant impact when gauging your weight as a candidate for a senior position.

When looking for the right course, don't rush. Allow yourself WEEKS of research, even if it means asking seemingly irrelevant questions.

With the more expensive MBA options comes the possibility of studying with executives working in Fortune 500 companies. Your exposure to experience and opportunities increases dramatically, creating a more valuable network – and this is critical to your future. If you still believe that networking doesn't matter, then I must disappoint you: networking is one of the most important elements of the MBA.

Samir travelled from India to the USA to study full time in one of the top universities. That required a lot of sacrifices, as his wife remained at home. On his return, he secured a position of General Manager in an oil company. When the oil crisis hit, his company shut down and initially it looked like the whole sacrifice was pointless. However, Samir found a job as a Finance Director in one of the largest delivery companies in the world, thanks to an MBA colleague who worked there.

How to choose a school

Start by defining the type of MBA you are interested in. This can take a long time if you do it properly. Talk to everyone, ask questions on LinkedIn, find friends who've already done the course, contact senior management. In short, gain as much of the real-person input as possible. The main criteria should be your planned career and what drives you in life.

Another vital factor is the acceptance of your MBA in your home country. Some Middle Eastern students are staying away from distance-learning modules because not all employers accept them. The best advice is to ask around. When looking for my course, I spoke to several head-hunters (specialist recruiters) who saw me as a future client and gave me plenty of advice.

A good indicator of the level of the course you'll be joining is the selection process. I would be wary of approaching an MBA with no entry exams or interviews and would recommend avoiding these. They are designed to cash in on you and give you a title to update your LinkedIn profile. If you really want to get something from the course, make sure that everyone who applies is *not* accepted.

Once you know the type of MBA, focus on the format. Studying full-time is not possible for most candidates, and here the situation gets more complicated. I would advise focusing on two areas.

1. Travelling. Can you afford to travel for weekends to attend an EMBA? When I say 'afford', I'm not just thinking of the hotel expenses but asking you to consider whether your family situation permits it. If you have no significant commitments limiting you, and your partner understands, then go for it. The deeper the immersion in weekend sessions, the more you will gain.

2. Work commitments. The MBA is about progression, not regression, so make sure you don't compromise your existing career. Are you a member of a larger team and is your employer willing to let you go as long as someone covers for you? Go for the Executive option. Are you a one-man-band who simply would not be in a position to delegate? Then go for distance learning.

Once you've decided on the type and format, the list of possible courses starts to look more manageable.

Excellent and well done! Now the real work begins when your mind is suddenly swamped with new worries, chiefly about money!

Let us look at some of them together in the next chapter.

Applying

You may be surprised to learn that the application is not as simple as completing a set of forms and paying the course fees.

Classes tend to be small, so the process of selecting candidates can be quite harsh. As a rule of thumb, the more prestigious schools will be much fussier and there is a good reason for that. Upon graduating, the alumni carry the name of the school with them and must be worthy of respect. In short, the school remains a top one if it admits only top candidates in the first place.

In most cases it is unlikely that you will have to attend an interview, but you will be asked for a CV and the reasons behind your decision to join the MBA. Something like 'I think the degree will help me in life' will land your file in the bin. Universities are looking for driven individuals with career plans and concrete expectations.

There is an excellent reason for the limited number of interviews. As some of my colleagues learned, the pace of the course is demanding; if you don't fit, or your experience and drive are insufficient, then you will simply resign. The dropout rate can be high and EVERY person I met who approached the MBA as a 'let's give it a go' exercise never completed it.

Experience: Extremely helpful. I write on that matter separately later in the guide.

Education: Students without GCSEs will have to prove they meet a certain standard in English and Maths. If that is your case, start the process by finding a course which can provide that. A Bachelor's degree is usually a minimum requirement.

Most universities want to ensure that their students have an appropriate level of knowledge and experience and have an entry exam, called the Graduate Management Admission Test (GMAT). There are courses which can prepare you for this but, if you've genuinely been a manager for three years, I would advise you to try the exam first. There are plenty of examples of the paper available online, so you can form your own opinion about whether you are ready to take it.

If you already studied abroad, but your diploma is not recognised in the UK, NARIC (https://www.naric.org.uk/naric/) may be able to compare your qualifications and skills. It is an excellent place to start; NARIC performs this function on behalf of the UK government, and most schools accept their certificates.

Language: Most top-ranking MBAs are taught in English. If it is not your first language, you will have to prove your efficiency by taking a recognised test. In Europe, I recommend going for International English Language Testing System (IELTS) which is accepted by almost all universities (and by that I mean that I have not found a single one which does not accept it).

A word of warning: MBA students should be able to understand academic jargon. The articles and books you'll study will be written mainly by academics, and your assignments and written exams will have to meet this standard. It is not the same as 'normal' English, so make sure you feel comfortable with it and consider some preparatory courses.

Application: An online application is the most common method and your chosen school will send you a list of the required paperwork. You may need recommendations from two people, one of whom is a professional (director level) with whom you have worked. These people are likely to be contacted by the university, so choose them carefully!

You may also be asked to write a short essay or attend a web-based meeting. The point is not to stress you but to test your openness and personality. I suggest you show your strengths, smile and be confident. I know it is easier said than done, but you will need to do this throughout the whole course.

Common worries

When I talk to potential seekers of management knowledge, I always discover that money is a frequent cause for concern. The worry is typically split across the following.

Finding the money for the course:
If you have already crossed this bridge, congratulations! If you are still thinking about it, start with a pencil in your hand. Yes, you will have to write down some things again…

The cost of an MBA varies significantly but you already understand how important it is to choose the right school. At the time of writing, the cheapest option in the UK stands at £6,200 for the whole course – rising to £78,500 at the top end. Believe me when I say that there is a value behind the more expensive ones; an expert will not share their knowledge for nothing, and you want to be taught by experts.

Self-funding: Apart from the scenario where you actually have the money in the bank, this can be a block for many students. If you are considering a loan, realistically assess your ability to pay it off. Do not overestimate how quickly your earnings will grow after the course and be aware that the older you are, the less significant the increase may be as you may already be earning a good salary. Research your industry and talk to senior management in your company.

Beware: this is a frequent trap for many students. They assume a salary increase of 25% immediately after obtaining the MBA but reality quite often doesn't follow that thinking. Yes, you will earn more, but your higher qualification still needs 'selling' and very rarely translates into an immediate increase. I once spoke to someone who was convinced that they would have a pay rise of 30% straight after completing the course; when we calculated how much that would be, it turned out that the industry they worked in simply wasn't paying that much.

So be realistic but don't give up if you cannot find the funds. Keep on reading.

Being sponsored: This is a very common way of amassing the necessary money and you may be surprised how frequently it happens. There are a lot of companies that want to invest in their staff. Approach your boss about sponsorship; however, think about your approach because it can backfire spectacularly if you don't do it properly.

Some golden nuggets of advice are:

Time it. Be patient. Imagine that someone is asking you for a significant commitment: you wouldn't like to be pressurised, so plan accordingly. Unfortunately there are very few shortcuts in life, if any, so steel yourself for a strategical rather than tactical approach. If you are thinking of starting a course within six months, that may be too soon for your sponsor. They also have to time their approach and allocate that expense in a budget.

Mention your academic intentions to your boss during your meetings. If your manager is not the person who will ultimately make a decision, find out whether they feel comfortable with approaching their superior about your case. This is very important, as your line manager (let's say it's the Sales Director) may want to keep you. They will assure you that they will do anything required to get your sponsorship, but if the decision-maker is the Managing Director with whom they have a complicated relationship, then 'selling' the concept may be difficult. If that's the case, I would advise approaching the Sales Director and asking if they would be okay with you going directly to the Managing Director. This allows them to graciously grant you that 'privilege' and, at the same time, gives you a direct line of communication.

The MBA should not be a target; it is a tool for reaching a goal. Your company will not benefit from your title alone, so don't sell it as the ultimate aim. What is quite often missed by those applying for the course is that the diploma itself will not change anything, and your organisation will not benefit from it. You can claim that your motivation will increase, but it is a high price for boosting someone's drive – and senior management will most likely decline. Continue reading and take this advice seriously.

Do your homework. If your business is expanding by buying other players in the market, then you may want to explain to your bosses that you see a need in the future for having senior managers familiar with the company's culture, who could take care of the newly-acquired units. If the business is still developing, you may want to ask about plans for the next ten years and suggest areas where there will be a need for someone in a senior position who understands the industry.

Talk to HR. Most large companies put aside money for training and are frustrated by a lack of suitable candidates willing to tap into that resource. As with all the advice, leave yourself plenty of time for 'planting seeds'. It may take several months for the Human Resource Director to talk to someone in your department and join the dots. I'm not saying that this is the way things *should* be, but in reality that is how they *are*.

Most importantly, don't put forward any conditions straight away. It will cost your company a lot of money to sponsor you and, for the most part, their decision will rely on your personality. If you come across as abrupt and impatient, they will not see it as an investment. It is acceptable to negotiate, but only when the process has been agreed in principle.

Understand your sponsor. This advice is quite often missed and is absolutely critical for your future. It is one thing to complete an MBA, but totally different to capitalise on it. The questions below will give you an idea about how to approach this point.

- *Is your company looking for a new wave of senior management?*
- *Could you form part of that wave?*
- *Is there an exciting development in the near future where your new skills could be applied?*

Even if you're in a company that doesn't seem to be growing, it is vital to understand senior management as perhaps they are looking to implement a succession plan,. That means they will be looking for someone to run the company after they have happily retired to the nearest golf course.

I once spoke to someone who complained that he didn't stand a chance of getting any money from the board as they were all old and very thrifty. When he eventually approached one of the directors, he was surprised to learn that most board members were planning to retire within the next decade and were worried about the future structure of the company. It was a family enterprise and being careful with budgets was a natural part of the routine, but within a few months the person was offered a course (with some caveats).

And this brings us to another point.

The process from the point of view of the sponsor

Typically there will be a budget somewhere for staff training but the cost of the MBA will likely exceed it, so don't bet on simply walking into an executive's office and leaving with a cheque.

There is no doubt that your sponsor will start drawing immediate benefits from your course, but these benefits may be intangible in the initial stages. You may be more motivated, you may start offering advice or revising some parts of the operation, but in few cases will you be able to improve the whole organisation straight away. And that is fine; be patient.

At the same time, share all the relevant knowledge you discover. Not only will you be able to contribute, you will reassure those senior to you of the value of the course. When you need some extra time off, or perhaps a helping hand, they may look on you more favourably.

It is also true that by the time you've graduated, your knowledge may already have started translating into tangible results such as higher sales, reduced costs due to restructuring, and more contracts and improved relationships with customers. You will become someone of great value.

Therein lies a challenge for your manager: if they think that you're considering leaving the company after the course to cash in on your new, shiny diploma, your application for funding has no chance of becoming anything more than a bin liner. They will be looking to safeguard their investment and may seek a written agreement with you. Take the initiative and suggest it yourself. This will encourage them to take you seriously – but don't destroy your advantage by laying out the terms at this stage. Let your manager think about it and make suggestions first. This will make them feel in control of the process; they can even claim it as their initiative. That's good. Don't worry – you are still at the centre of the process.

Typically, bosses will want an assurance from you that you will pay off the course if you drop out. That's common sense, so don't be surprised. Check with your school what happens in these circumstances and how much of a refund they would be able to offer. Many courses are flexible; you may be able to commit to a lot without endangering your own finances too much.

Life can have many turns and twists and this allows for effective management of them.

Robert's children were in their twenties when he decided that finally he had enough time to start the MBA. He was able to pay for the course with his own money and, in the process of looking for the right school, he had to decide between two almost identical options. One of them offered to 'freeze' his grades for a year in addition to refunding fees on a module-by-module basis if he took an academic break,.

When his daughter called a year later with the happy news that she was pregnant, Robert wanted to support her for the first twelve months after the baby was born. He called the university; not only was he able to move the course, but they also refunded him for the future units that he would miss. He would pay for them when he returned.

It is a happy story, but Robert confessed to me that he initially felt like a cheapskate asking for a refund. His diligence paid off, however – so invest time in looking at the small print.

Your director may want to keep you after the MBA to fully realise your potential. The exact negotiations will be unique to you – it is impossible to cover all the variables here – but you must think strategically. Remember that your company will only invest if they see a long-running scenario and time commitment, so you must understand their motivation.

The best way is to take their investment as an expression of their confidence in you and a statement of future commitment.

Most critically, be warned if you don't like the company you are working in and are thinking that the MBA will allow you to 'skip the ship'. This is a short-sighted approach and can create a toxic environment. The MBA is a great experience but there is also a lot of pressure. During my time on the course, there were four people who treated it as a means of escape and gave it up eventually, unable to combine their aspirations with reality.

Make sure you start in the right place where you feel comfortable. As a rule of thumb, I would suggest working on a retention period that mirrors the commitment time, i.e. if your course takes two years, that should be your maximum retention time. Anything less and you are in a great place.

Previous experience

Do you need to have had some work experience? My answer to this question is 'yes'. There are many MBA courses where you can enrol without prior work experience, but I would advise caution with these.

Unless you're a full-time student who wants to continue into MBA to join a consultancy company, work experience is very relevant. Consultancy companies are designed to expose bright graduates to real-life business cases and nurture them via mentorship, so they approach the process from a different angle (education first, experience later).

The topics that will be taught during the course are multi-faceted and will inevitably touch on ethical standards. It is easy to make a decision which is beneficial financially in the short run, but it is an art to recognise the fallacy of a short-term approach. The MBA gives you tools to manage a longer view. If you've never hired or fired, made money and (more importantly) lost it, you may not pick up on the most important lessons.

There is an ongoing debate about whether management is a real profession. At the end of the day, lawyers work within the boundaries of the law, doctors are bound by a code, but managers have no formal code of conduct as they must embrace an ever-shifting environment. There is a particular art to the job; only experiencing it yourself will make you fully appreciate the content of the course.

The MBA appeared in the United States in the early twentieth century as a way of approaching management scientifically; ever since then discussion has been raging about whether this is possible.

Irrespective of your opinion on that subject, it is clear that you will need some experience.

PART II SCHOOL TIME

So you've finally decided on the course and emails from the school are flooding your inbox. You are excited and promise to always aim for the highest marks.

Slow down ... that's great, but be aware that a reality check is just around the corner. By all means buy the university T-shirt and some new pens, but remember you probably don't need to scour bookshops for the best-selling books on management. Not yet, anyway.

First steps

You will most likely be inundated with new rules for studying, especially if you have spent some time outside academia. The primary advice is:

Get the basics right. Pay attention to that warning. Things like learning how to reference according to Harvard rules may seem irrelevant, but they will help you build foundations for good grades rather than merely meeting deadlines.

Mohammed skimmed the first section on academic writing due to a busy work schedule. The rules seemed obvious and not business-oriented. When writing assignments at the end of the first module, he had to reference all of his sources;

41

it took him a couple of days to write the main body of his work but nearly two weeks to reference the books and articles he had used. Moreover, his work was scored low because it lacked the required structure. Having learnt his lesson, he spent extra time going through the rules once again.

Remember, there are no shortcuts. Later in your course you can decide which elements are essential but you must get the basics right. Leaving notes in books, or doing a full reference list as you work, may be seem to impede the speed of your writing but remember Aesop's tale of the hare and the tortoise!

Work with your colleagues

The MBA is about networking. Irrespective of the knowledge you are about to embrace, this will be essential in your post-MBA life. Engage on as many platforms as possible and be open with your colleagues. There WILL be a time when you rely on their help and assistance.

When I joined my MBA course, I was invited to the chat-group on WhatsApp. Initially it seemed a waste of time, but I joined to benefit from forming good relationships. During the first assignments and seminars, only I and a handful of others instigated discussions, shared material and generally kept things going, so the benefits of having that platform were minimal. Even so, I persisted.

One year later, during a hectic period of work-related travels, visits, plans and projects, as well as looking for a new house, I discovered that I didn't have the usual time for my revision. And this is where the magic happened. The WhatsApp group has been gaining momentum and people were feeding information to it. Instead of spending hours trawling through formats and rules, I could scroll through the chat and get the gist of what had to be done.

Was that lazy? Perhaps. Did I do a quality job? I would like to think that I did, but most certainly via a substantial shortcut.

The alternative was to compromise in another area. The reality of life is that there are only twenty-four hours in a day and unfortunately we all have to sleep sometimes, so creating an environment in which you can lean on others is necessary. I must stress that I did the revision by myself. I didn't do too badly in that exam – but I would definitely have done a lot worse if it hadn't been for others' help.

My colleagues, and I used every available tool at our disposal with shared notes on OneNote pages. It helped us to bond and many (even those who didn't have time to contribute) were grateful.

The MBA is a hectic course; no matter how much time you think you have, you will run out of it at some stage. Life is not about beating the course all by yourself, and doing it with others does not take anything away from your achievement. Quite the contrary – you will discover that it actually enhances it. Just don't forget to thank those who help you. It makes a remarkable difference!

Achieving a balance

The balancing act is a difficult one, but you must remember that it is a movement rather than a fixed state. What I mean by that is that you will continually sway from one extreme to another and only occasionally achieve equilibrium.

That is fine. Initially I spent a lot of my time regretting things I couldn't do instead of focusing on those that I could do. Do not repeat my mistake. It's only natural that you will sometimes 'wing it' (an English phrase meaning that you made hardly any preparations and had to rely on your intelligence). Throughout my professional life, I met plenty of high-level executives who were clearly winging it, and a certain amount of practice is needed to make this look effortless. More on that subject later – just don't stress too much.

Set yourself boundaries but be ready to break them. Let me elaborate. You must draw some 'red lines' which you should not cross, such as: 'I will still play golf but instead of every weekend, I will do it on the first Saturday of the month', or 'Sundays are family time'.

Even more important is understanding that you actually CAN cross them if required. Do not get too stressed by the fact that you didn't find a lot of time during the week and are running late. Your peace of mind and mental health are most important; if one of those fails, the whole course will become a pain and you will not enjoy it.

When there was a lecture on Monday and a seminar on Thursday, for which I needed to prepare, I found it challenging not only to read the material but also watch the lecture and familiarise myself with the articles and books required as a minimum. I was getting up at 3am to study before going to work. I cut out the gym entirely and in the evenings was so stressed and tired that I barely found time for my family. This, in turn, irritated me even more so I would get up already angry at myself.

45

What I didn't realise was that there would eventually be time to catch up with everything; that required fresh thinking. As soon as I realised that some lecturers basically read from their slides, I downloaded the lectures onto the phone and listened to them while commuting to work. That allowed me to fully utilise two hours every day (I work in London, so there is always heavy traffic and long journeys).

When it came to reading, I switched from driving the car to taking trains and planes for business trips whenever possible. I visited customers and production for most of the week, so that freed up some hours. I also started planning my visits better and trying to stay in hotels one night a week. At first I felt like I was cheating my family and compromising on the red lines, but when I was with my family I was more relaxed and actually a better father than before. The red line became orange, and everyone was happier for it.

Time management here is key. If you plan your week, you'll find gaps you can fill with going out for dinner or watching a movie with your children. If, on the other hand, you tend to 'play it by ear', you will most likely find your levels of stress increasing.

Most of my colleagues (just like me) deleted some of their social accounts where they found themselves scrolling for hours and doing nothing productive. Others deleted the apps from their phones and logged in on their laptops to catch up. This meant they actually had to allocate time and they avoided the trap of mindless phone-staring. Whichever option you go for, make sure that you consciously review your existing habits.

Time commitment

The MBA is not for the faint-hearted and will be challenging. Whichever model you decide on, whether it is an executive one with frequent physical sessions, or distance learning with students attending only workshops and online seminars, it will demand all of your time. And more.

Some of the universities list time requirements for their courses. Fifteen, twenty or twenty-five hours a week may seem doable but these hours refer to the time required to do the bare minimum; additional reading will most certainly consume more of your time. Critically, any preparations for the exams or assignments will create peak demands requiring high concentrations of study time.

When you negotiate terms and conditions with your sponsor, ask them to allocate time off for your academic work.

Having three days off before a deadline for an assignment may seem very little, but it will be invaluable when, having had four coffees, you still have a bibliography to do, your partner is cross with you because you haven't gone out anywhere in ages, and your kids are screaming.

Family and social life
This is a very important aspect that you must address before embarking on the MBA trip. You need your family to support your decision; they must understand that, whereas previously you were able to cook or take them somewhere, these times will be under revision during the MBA.

Relax. Your life will not stop. You will still be able to enjoy your other passions and go out with your partner.

The key phrases for this section are 'managing expectations' and 'time and attention management'. You will have to change your habits. One of the most significant surprises for most students relates to the sudden inability to continue streaming their favourite boxsets in the evening, or to have a glass of wine every other day, or go fishing at weekends.

Start respecting your time and allocate it as if it were your most precious commodity, because that's exactly what it is. That is so important that I will actually repeat it: ***Time is your most precious commodity.***

Prioritise your time with loved ones and think about which parts of your life can be put on hold temporarily or outsourced. There are plenty of small companies that offer shirt-ironing and house-cleaning services, and their costs can be low.

Ask yourself:

- *Do you really have to meet Geoff for that weekly round of golf?*
- *Will Sasha be upset if you don't meet her this week for a cup of tea?*

Both of these are important, and it may be important to sustain them, but the question here is 'at what level'.

When I joined the MBA, I started getting up at 3am to travel to the office and study before everyone came in. I would still go home at a reasonable time to be with my wife and kids, but the most significant compromise for me was the change to my evening routine: I started going to sleep at 7.30pm, at the same time as my little son. I had to embrace the lifestyle of a three year old, but this allowed me to find three hours every day to study. By the time the weekend arrived, I'd done most of the academic minimum and could 'afford' to have a day off.

Pablo didn't have a family but was travelling a lot between countries as a senior salesman for Middle Asia, which meant finding some quality study time was tricky. When he joined the MBA course, his first task was to rearrange his travel itinerary to reduce it to a minimum, and to try and stay in a hotel for more than one night. This meant he would not see his friends back home for a long time but allowed him to find the necessary time to study.

The list of examples is very long but, critically, you will have to re-evaluate your priorities.

Start practising attention and time management before the MBA so you've really sharpened your skills when you start. They are not the same things, so make sure you've done plenty of research on both.

It is a given that you will run out of time at some point. It is down to you to establish the frequency of these events. Plan your day, including your breaks, and communicate your plans to someone so you feel guilty if you don't stick to the schedule.

I started listening to audiobooks on efficiency and implemented as much of their advice as possible. There are some seriously great publications on the subject (*Productivity Ninja* being one of them – I am not paid for endorsement but enjoyed it immensely), so start working on that now. If you feel that all of this is forced or artificial, then believe me when I say that you will change your mind quickly.

Use technology

The time of spending days in the library is long gone. As much as I still enjoy spending time there, the library now goes with me. You can log in remotely and read a book from your tablet. Make sure you use all the tools available.

Voice-typing – I found this very helpful, as my electronic phone assistant was 'noting down' my thoughts for assignments. Yes, there is still plenty to rectify but this technology improves every month.

RefWorks – and other programmes available online will help you with your Harvard referencing.

Word processor – most word-processing software has a referencing option built-in. It will save you hours of tedious tracing back of the literature you used. I advise spending a couple of hours studying this option if you're not yet familiar with it.

Social platforms – invaluable when it comes to exchanging information. Our WhatsApp group saved me on many occasions. I personally found the University's platform too cumbersome, but it was only a few days before we had a separate group on a messaging app.

Collaboration tools – make sure that you maximise the use of devices such as Microsoft SharePoint and similar tools. Sharing files, notes, pictures and even links to interesting articles is a must if you are to gain the most from the course. It can be tough, so make sure you have access to resources.

Google Scholar – ever heard of Google? Of course, you have. Now you are going to meet Google Scholar. This search engine indexes full texts or metadata of scholarly resources across numerous disciplines. It lists peer-reviewed academic journals, books and articles, as well as theses and dissertations. The Great Library of Alexandria was said to hold up to 400,000 scrolls but Google Scholar supposedly contains more than 350 million documents (this is unofficial data as Google does not publish any numbers).

Pushing the hours

Irrespective of the improvements you can implement in your life, there will come a time when twenty-four hours becomes insufficient. And then what?

Take care of yourself. Eat healthily. Look for marginal gains.

This is actually a fundamental concept, which I recommend you embrace when thinking of the MBA. Those familiar with cycling will know it, but for the rest of us (including myself previously), I need to bring up the story of the British cycling team which was performing so poorly at one point that their sponsor refused to sell them merchandise because they were worried it would affect sales.

Sir Dave Brailsford was hired to change that and he started looking for marginal gains in EVERYTHING. Bike seats were redesigned, electrically heated shorts were bought for the riders to maintain perfect muscle temperatures, and various materials were tested aerodynamically to find a 1% gain in everything. The riders were even taught how to wash their hands properly to avoid food poisoning and catching a cold.

The team became the best in the world and started winning medals in competitions where they'd never achieved anything! The positive effect of 'aggregation of marginal gains' was proved in real life. Sir Dave Brailsford brought his cycling experience into those changes – but what many people don't know is that he is also an MBA graduate.

Marginal gains are the small sacrifices you can make which, if combined, should add up to large ones.

For the first year of the MBA, I stopped going out. I'd never partied hard, but I assumed that going dry wouldn't hurt me. And I was right! My sleep improved, and I was able to maintain a better focus for longer. It was a small change but definitely helped.

Christine cancelled her streaming subscription. It was a significant change for her initially, but helped her to find up to four hours a week extra. Instead of relaxing in front of the TV, she walked for fifteen minutes instead. Those four hours over the year added up to more than two hundred in total.

Mohammed felt that his whole world was crumbling when he received a promotion after joining the MBA. His manager was so impressed with having an ambitious employee that he instantly recognised Mohammed's drive and elevated him to Regional Sales Executive. Despite the new opportunities and significantly better money, Mohammed felt he couldn't cope with the workload and the requirements of the MBA.

Furthermore, he felt that a failure on the course would mean losing his new status. At some stage, however, he discovered that a lot of his administrative duties could be done by a junior member of the team. His manager praised him for taking the initiative and Mohammed finally had the time he needed to study.

You will push the hours and find yourself in strange cafes at random hours. I once sat in a layby taking part in the seminar with my laptop hooked up to the power socket of an empty coach, which had stopped there for rest. Do not be afraid to ask for help!

We waste a lot of time in our lives and the MBA helps to take stock of that fact. I suggest that you write down everything you do during the day and the time it takes. Assess the areas where you can make marginal gains – and eliminate checking the football results ten times a day.

Finding help

Do not be afraid to ask others to help you. Somewhere in your organisation is a person who knows more about a subject than you do. And if your company is not a large corporation, then you've probably met someone in your professional life who can spend half an hour explaining a problem.

Here is why: these people are passionate about their jobs and love talking about them. They will be able to support theory with practical examples. Imagine someone asked you about your job; you would be only too happy to enlighten them.

Do not be ashamed of saying 'I don't know'. I actually improved a lot of relationships with my colleagues after admitting they knew more. You don't lose face, you don't admit ignorance, so stop being shy.

Mike was an Operations Manager with decades of experience in his field but was struggling with the SaaS concept. His company decided he would head the project to implement one of the solutions which, in addition to his MBA, really pushed him and caused a lot of stress. Finally, encouraged by his fellow students, Mike asked for help. He knew that the IT person in the company had some understanding of the concept and went to see her. To his amazement, she not only explained the concept but confessed she would like to be the lead. That afternoon Mike sat with his Managing Director and suggested this, thus gaining not only strong technical support but also recognition from senior management that he could appoint the right people. Mike continued to oversee the project and soon became an authority in his company on the subject.

Sound incredible? I can assure you that Mike went through a personal crisis at the beginning. I don't know what happened to the IT expert but, knowing Mike, I'm sure she received all the necessary recognition.

YouTube and social media

Okay, I know that social media isn't a serious academic source of knowledge, but I can't count the times when I found someone on YouTube who had uploaded a video explaining a problem that I could not previously understand.

When I went for the Finance option on my MBA, I was initially so out of depth on certain subjects that I read through every possible article and book to catch up. What I needed was someone who could simplify the complicated language. And YouTube is full of those people.

I will forever remain indebted to an American MBA graduate who talked about a Capital Asset Pricing Model; he not only showed me the basics but also got me hooked on the subject. In his twenty-minute video, a French banker revealed a simple way to read financial statements; I can honestly admit that without his help I probably would have struggled. At the same time, I also approached two directors in my division with accounting backgrounds on the same matter.

TEDx has a wide range of talks. I recommend setting yourself a target of watching one every other day, or every day if you have time. These videos are designed to be less than eighteen minutes long and are delivered by experts.

A vital part of the MBA is opening your mind to new ideas and concepts; getting immersed in LinkedIn articles (as long as you do it critically) can only benefit you. So don't shy away from spending time on the internet browsing through non-academic materials.

Feeling alone

This is a familiar feeling for most of the MBA students. Living '*la vida loca*' is not for everyone but, if you found the courage to join the course, don't be daunted by those moments when you find no-one can understand you. Indeed, unless someone has gone through this experience already, it is difficult to comprehend why anyone would put so much pressure on themselves.

You must realise that you are not alone. Others on the course will be going through the same wild juggling act. Network with them and soon you'll discover friends in parts of the world you never knew you had. Make sure that you keep in touch with your fellow students; just like you, many of them will most likely be travelling the world and at some stage your paths may cross. Make an effort to go out to meet them.

When I learnt that one of my colleagues was staying for one night in a hotel in Gatwick, I jumped into the car and drove for nearly two hours to meet him. It was after a twelve-hour day – and not a good one. Typically for the UK it rained, and I arrived in the evening so only one restaurant was open. Despite all that, we had a drink and talked until we were asked to leave. I cannot count the times this person later inspired me to work harder. The bond was formed and I wasn't the only one on the road any more.

Coping with the avalanche

An avalanche starts with a slow build-up of snow over a long period. When the weight reaches a critical point, a sudden event (such as a loud noise or vibration) disturbs the excess weight, which in turn triggers snow to roll down the mountain. As the avalanche heads downwards, it builds up, picking up everything on its path.

Stories about MBA studies are remarkably similar.

Marco worked for his company as a middle manager for more than five years before he approached his boss about the MBA course. After some deliberation, the boss agreed to co-fund the course. It was the right decision; after only one year, Marco started contributing towards the creation of new products, and the boss felt he should be rewarded with more responsibility. Marco was promoted to the Head of Development with ten employees reporting to him.

This is a real-life story and at first sounds like an excellent result, but Marco suddenly found himself in a new, unfamiliar job with a lot of responsibility just when the pace of the MBA course intensified.

The avalanche had started moving and Marco did the right thing. He sat down with a cup of tea and a pencil to plan. He counted the time he needed for the university work, his family and his new responsibilities in one column. In the second column, he wrote what was realistically possible and identified (unsurprisingly) that his new position would 'consume' more than seventy hours per week, something that was not achievable. He then asked which of his new responsibilities could delegated to someone else and managed to shave ten hours off his workload.

The sixty hours were still far from ideal. Having already gained some knowledge from the MBA, Marco started looking critically at the requirements of the new position and what he actually expected of himself. He quickly realised that that other Heads of Departments were working on average forty hours a week; he had added twenty extra hours unnecessarily by trying to cling to some of his old responsibilities. Now the end figure looked like an achievable one.

By letting go of his previous position, Marco allowed others to progress and, despite the initial need to mentor them and teach them the ropes, he constructed a manageable workload.

This story is true but, as with most inspirational tales, it is told from a positive angle. In reality, Marco felt like his head was about to explode; he wanted to quit and once he even cried. No, Marco is not me, but I can confirm that I was in the same position many times. It is only natural but the MBA will give you the confidence to deal with these problems.

Firstly, you must understand that your thinking will (and must) switch from detail-oriented to strategic; to progress your career, you must stop worrying too much about details. There will certainly be other people who are only too anxious to do that for you as it will help them progress. And the more responsible the organisation you work for, the more focus it will have on creating future generations of management.

MBA and your career

How will the MBA influence my career?

That is an excellent question. The answer, as always, depends on the reality of your situation. You may be surprised to learn that many students initial expectations are realised during their time at the university.

By joining the course, I was hoping to build foundations for my future career; I most definitely did not expect it to take off during the MBA. Moreover, it did so in an unexpected direction, and I discovered an internal push towards the development of relationships with customers. I started as a Head of the Technical and Quality department in my division, but within two years I had also embraced the responsibilities of Account Executive and was involved in planning supply chains for parts of the business. I was part of teams putting together costings for multiple tenders, and supported all the business units of my division.

Hang on, you may say; that sounds almost *too* good. You would be right. My progress wasn't all due to my new knowledge (although that helped immensely). It happened because of the change in my attitude and approach towards problems. The necessity to juggle multiple tasks turned me into someone who finally started to listen, became attuned to the needs of others and could voice my opinions to senior management.

My experience is not unique; almost everyone I spoke to during my research for this book went through similar changes. One close friend decided to leave her native country and immigrate to Canada in pursuit of the job she loved.

So, what do you need to do to make sure you benefit from the course?

Firstly, you must have a plan. I like to work on a three-level time horizon of five, ten and fifteen years, but this is a personal preference so you may go for a different timescale. Make sure that your plan is broad enough but is not too rich in details, as they will only complicate achieving it.

Secondly, start using your knowledge. There is no point in studying if you don't translate learning into life. By doing that, you will elevate yourself to a new level.

Thirdly, realise that the MBA certificate will not change your life. This is very important in getting value out of the course, so I will repeat it: *The MBA itself will not change your life.* Instead, your level of commitment will change you and turn you in an absolute volcano of energy if you let it. The twists may be unexpected, so keep an open mind.

On the other hand, if you find that you can't spend a night reading about telecommunications systems in China or agri-tech development in Africa, I would suggest the MBA may not be the best course for you.

Chris was an account manager in the UK division of a content-producing company when he started his MBA. Six months into the course, the German head office decided to restructure and closed the UK division. Undeterred, Chris found a new job. Just before starting it, he received a phone call from Hamburg to say that senior management had decided to retain some of the more profitable business and opted for creating an office in London. With his MBA aspirations and knowledge of customers, Chris seemed a perfect candidate to head one of the departments. That was not his original intention but, recognising opportunity, Chris accepted the offer and asked for an increased salary.

Again, I must add some reality to the above picture and point out that Chris went through a rollercoaster of emotions during this time – but the course gave him the confidence to risk coming back to his old employer.

Talking a different language

During one of the master classes at my university, someone quoted the example of his last interview. When discussing a business problem, he didn't have to lean on his MBA knowledge but realised after the process that the language he had used was very different from the one he'd used before the MBA.

He expressed himself in similar terms to the people who interviewed him; by doing so, he was unknowingly stressing his professional background. He landed the job, and I am sure he went far.

The moral of this story is that, if you want the MBA to be meaningful for your career, you must embrace all levels of education. Start talking the talk. Use examples you learned during studies. Challenge the received wisdom in your organisations. All of this must happen to allow you to flourish

What about the 'two-year curse'?

There is a misconception among those with the MBA under their belts that most of us leave companies within two years after graduating; I was told it by someone who left after twenty-five months. This is not necessarily true; I have not found a study that confirms this statistic. However, most certainly your eyes will open. I can guarantee that your horizons will broaden and you may become interested in other pursuits, even outside your current industry.

Coincidentally, three months after this conversation, that person left his position as Commercial Director in my group to embrace the challenge of being Managing Director somewhere else. This only shows the hunger for an adventure which ought to be burning in you by the end of the MBA.

.

Last word

Hopefully, you now have a better idea about the challenges and rewards of the MBA. Make sure you've done enough research before approaching universities or seeking funds. These stages are under-valued but, once you've started the course, it will be difficult to change schools so make sure you are happy with the format, distance and staff (yes, ask for the names of the key programme directors and Google them and their achievements).

You want to be inspired! The MBA will cost you a lot of money and effort, so you're entitled to expect only the best. Remember that you will have to push for that, so get ready to network. Most importantly, trust in yourself and always look towards the final goal!

We have discussed formats, money, worries and time. I have been as honest as possible, and my experience matches that of my colleagues. Ultimately, you must feel comfortable with your decision and choose the format and school that suits you best, but my main advice is be honest with yourself and work hard.

The MBA can be compared to a journey during which you will gain a new perspective on the world, your work and yourself. As with all transitional experiences it is challenging but, if you persist, you will emerge with a great skillset and a new mindset.